301.44 SAN 1977

Sandler, Martin W.
The way we lived : a
photographic record of

THE WAY WE LIVED

THE WAY WE LIVED

A Photographic Record of Work in a Vanished America

Martin W. Sandler

Little, Brown and Company
BOSTON   TORONTO

For Scott, Laura, and Craig

FIRST EDITION
Second Printing
T 10/77

All photographs in this book not listed below are reproduced from the collection of the Library of Congress.

New Haven Colony Historical Society, pages 12, 70; Rhode Island Historical Society, page 71; Sandler Collection, pages ii, 48, 66–67, 97; Snow Library, Orleans, Massachusetts, page 31; Society for the Preservation of New England Antiquities, pages 33, 34–35, 36; Mrs. Porter Thayer, page 74; Vermont Historical Society, page 116; Whaling Museum, New Bedford, Massachusetts, pages 88, 118 (bottom).

Library of Congress Cataloging in Publication Data

Sandler, Martin W
  The way we lived.

  SUMMARY: Photographs and text depict various
occupations in the United States between the end of the
Civil War and the outbreak of World War I.
    1. Laboring and laboring classes—United States—
History—Pictorial works—Juvenile literature.
[1. Labor and laboring classes—History. 2. United
States—Social conditions—1865–1918] I. Title.
HD8072.S265   301.44'42'0973   77-10810
ISBN 0-316-77020-5

Published simultaneously in Canada
by Little, Brown & Company (Canada) Limited
BP
PRINTED IN THE UNITED STATES OF AMERICA

Acknowledgments

There are several people to whom I owe thanks for help in the preparation of this book: Gerald Kearns and LeRoy Bellamy of the Library of Congress; Shirley Green of Bethesda, Maryland; Daniel Lohnes of the Society for the Preservation of New England Antiquities; and Susan McCullough of the Brookline, Massachusetts, public schools.

I also wish to thank John Keller, Jordie Brener, and Robert Lowe of Little, Brown and Company. I am happy to count them as friends as well as colleagues. Finally, as is the case with all my projects, my wife, Carol Weiss Sandler, played a vital role in the conception and completion of this book.

Preface

A PHOTOGRAPH is a kind of miracle. There on a piece of paper, for example, is our mother exactly as she looked when she was a little girl. There, in another photograph, are people on a picnic some eighty-five years ago. Their features are so clear, the scene so well captured that they seem ready to move before our very eyes. Nothing records the past more accurately than do photographs. They show us how people lived, played, and worked in times long since gone by.

This is a book of photographs. More accurately, it is a book of photographs that show Americans at work about one hundred years ago. Almost all of the pictures were taken between the years 1880 and 1920. Photographers at that time used glass-plate negatives in their cameras. Photography was still in its infancy; cameras were large and bulky, and the glass negatives were not easy to handle—but they produced the clearest images ever taken.

It was a time when people were fascinated with having their picture taken. They would pose at every opportunity—in front of their homes, beside their work, on a Sunday stroll. If a photographer was taking a picture in front of a building, people would stick their heads out of windows to get into the picture. For many people it was their one chance to have their likeness recorded for all time.

Work has always been an important subject for the camera's eye. And Americans have always worked hard at a great variety of jobs. Many of the occupations shown in the photographs in this book no longer exist. Others still exist but are now done in very different ways. Some of those that still exist were then known by very different names. For example, in this book you will see photographs of draymen, dubbers, coopers, and breaker boys.

In the late 1880s and early 1900s, most people toiled at least ten hours a day, six days a week. And they did this fifty-one weeks a year. Most of their lives were spent at work. It was a time when most workers took great pride in their labor. Whether they were building the pilothouse of a steamboat or the facing of a large building, much attention was paid to every detail.

It was also a time when young people were given real tasks to do. In some occupations, like farming, their work was essential to their families' success. Tragically, it was also a period in which thousands of young people were forced, at very early ages, to work long hours in places like mines and factories.

As noted, the photographs in this book are from the period when glass negatives were used. It so happens that these were remarkable years in this country, for it was during this time that the coming of the machine began to make great changes in the way Americans moved about—and in the way they worked. Thus the photographs record not only how people worked but how work itself was changed for all time.

As you read through this book, look carefully at the photographs. Try to notice every detail. What do the signs say? What kinds of tools are the workers using? Do their expressions tell us anything about the way they felt?

Many of the locations where these photographs were taken are still much the same today, but our ways of working and daily lives are much different. Were the people more happy or less happy then? Who is to say? One thing is certain—this is the way we lived!

Contents

Logging

ONE OF THE BEST of the early American photographers was a man named Darius Kinsey. He was particularly interested in the life of the men in the northwestern logging camps. These men felled huge trees, sawed them into logs, and hauled them to the sawmills to be cut into lumber.

Logging was an extremely important industry in early America. Most houses and buildings were made of wood. Lumber was used up as quickly as it could be shipped from the sawmills to builders all over the country. Camps where logging was carried on were, for the most part, like small towns. They often included blacksmith and carpenter shops, a dining hall, a company store where the men could buy clothing and tobacco, and bunkhouses where the men slept. There were also stables and haysheds for the horses.

The life of a lumberjack, as loggers were often called, was not easy. Work continued from sunup to sundown. There were many dangers involved. Still, the forests of America rang with the sound of the chopper's ax and the log hauler's commands. And tens of thousands of board feet of precious lumber were made available every year for a growing nation.

It took a great deal of skill to chop through a huge tree and have it fall in the right place. Loggers used different kinds of axes for different kinds of tasks. Most often, however, they used a thick, heavy ax that would take out huge chips with each blow. Veteran choppers bragged that they could lay a coin on the ground and drop the largest of trees flush upon it. Many of them could.

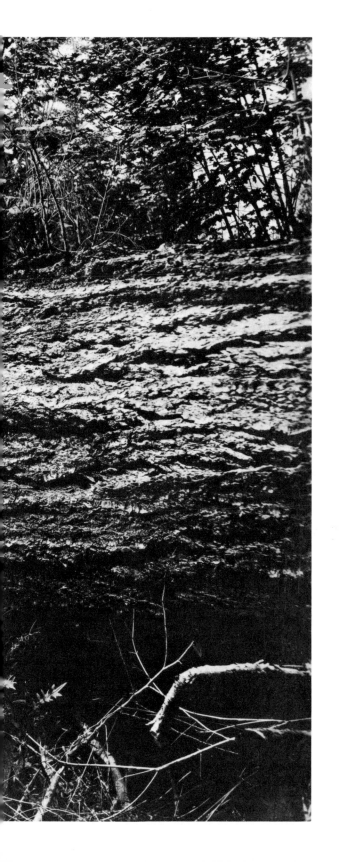

In His Own Words:
A SAWYER

OURS WAS a large logging camp. At any one time there were at least seventy men working there. Besides the foreman and his clerk, there was a cook and his assistant, a blacksmith, a saw filer, a carpenter, and two handymen.

The rest of the camp was divided into crews. There were choppers whose job it was to cut down the trees. There were sawyers, like myself, who sawed the felled trees into logs once they were on the ground. The skidders saw to it that the cut-up logs were hauled to the roads which led to the river or directly to the saw mill. Men called swampers kept the roads in good condition. Finally, there were crews of teamsters who cared for the horses and were in charge of hauling the logs.

We rolled out of our bunks at four o'clock every morning. At five o'clock we had breakfast and were at our work with the first rays of light. The work was hard and not without its share of dangers. The choppers were experts at dropping the trees just where they wanted them to fall. But sometimes a tree would crack and the upper part would drop straight to the ground causing all who were around to scramble for safety. In the winter frost and snow made the fallen logs very slippery, which resulted in many spills.

As I said, logging was hard work. But I enjoyed my years in the camp. Most of all, I loved being in the woods.

Adapted from an unpublished manuscript by Harvey W. Watson, 1910. (Mr. Watson was a logger in the state of Oregon.)

Once the fallen trees were cut into logs they were sent off to the sawmill to be made into lumber. Often they were hauled over specially built roads that led directly to the mill. In winter, water was poured over these roads. Huge loads could then be pulled over the ice.

In the spring the logs were often dumped into a nearby river and floated to the site of the sawmill. Workers hoisted the huge logs out of the river and rode the "Washington toothpicks" directly into the mill.

Farming

THROUGHOUT MOST of our history, farmers have been the backbone of American society. Most colonial Americans grew and harvested their own food. The opening of millions of acres of fertile land as the West was settled made the United States one of the greatest farming nations in the world. Even after the coming of the machine, when so many people went to work in factories and other industries, farmers still greatly outnumbered workers in any other occupation. In fact, as late as 1890 there were twice as many people employed on American farms as in any other occupation.

Farming has never been easy. Although songs and stories have tended to glorify life on the farm, American farmers have always had to deal with such problems as floods, windstorms, drought, and insects. Even the coming of farm machinery in the late 1800s was a mixed blessing. On one hand, it made farm life much easier. One machine could do the work of many people. And machines allowed American farmers to produce more food than was ever thought possible. On the other hand, many farmworkers found themselves being replaced by the new, efficient machinery.

Still, well into the 1900s, millions of Americans earned their living at one kind of farm work or another. And they did their jobs so well that they helped supply the whole world with food.

By the 1860s, the wooden plow, which had been used by generations of American farmers, had been replaced by stronger plows made of iron. The iron plow was one of the most important inventions in American history. It made it easier for settlers in regions never farmed before to turn over the soil and plant their all-important first crops.

Farm work was hard and the hours were long. But there were rewards to be found in working out-of-doors, close to the land. And there was a closeness in many farm families that came from meeting common problems together.

Today a large percentage of American farms are owned and operated by huge companies or corporations. In the late 1800s and early 1900s almost all American farms were family affairs. Everyone in the family had his or her tasks to do. Young people fed and watered the animals, milked the cows, and worked in the fields.

Then, as now, American farmers grew a great variety of crops. Some were native to certain regions of the country. In New England, for example, asparagus, cucumbers, and certain grades of tobacco were raised. Grapes, oranges, peaches, and pineapples were important crops in warm-weather states such as Florida, Georgia, and California. The farms of the Midwest supplied the world with corn, wheat, and other grains. Other crops were native to other regions.

No matter what the area, however, almost all American farmers needed to grow hay to feed their animals. In the beginning, hay harvesting was done totally by hand. A farmworker's skill was often measured by how large and tight a load he or she could pile on a wagon. As years passed new ways were developed. A horse-drawn device was introduced that helped farmers pile up stacks of hay. Finally huge machines were invented that cut, baled, and loaded the hay, all in one operation.

In the midwest, one of the most important farm operations took place when it came time to reap, or cut and harvest, the wheat. In the account that follows, a fourteen-year-old boy describes the farm at reaping time.

In His Own Words:
A FARM BOY

REAPING came about the twentieth of July, the hottest and dryest part of the summer. It was the most pressing work of the year. It demanded early rising for the men and it meant an all-day broiling over the kitchen stove for the women. The work went on inside and out from dawn until sunset. On many days the heat mounted to ninety-five in the shade.

Reaping was a full-grown man's job, but every boy was anxious to try his hand. When, at fourteen years of age, I was promoted from "bundle boy" to be one of the five hands to bind after the reaping, I went to my work with great joy.

I was short and broad-shouldered with large, strong hands. For the first two hours I easily held my own with the rest of the crew. But as the morning wore on and the sun grew hotter my enthusiasm dimmed. At noon we hurried to the house, surrounded the kitchen table and fell upon our boiled beef and potatoes. Then came a heavenly half-hour of rest on the cool grass with the shade of the trees. But alas—the "nooning," as we called it, was always cut short by father's word of sharp command, "Roll out, boys." All nature at this hour seemed to invite rest rather than work. Yet each of us must strain his tired muscles and bend his aching back to the harvest.

Supper came at five—and then at six we all went out again for another hour or two in the cool of the sunset. At last, father's cry, "Turn out! All hands, turn out!" Then slowly the horses moved toward the barn with lagging steps like weary warriors going into camp.

Adapted from *A Son of the Middle Border*, by Hamlin Garland, The Macmillan Company, 1917. (The Garland family farm was in Iowa.)

By the 1900s machines had changed almost every aspect of life in the United States. Nowhere was this truer than on the farm. In 1890 there were about twenty million horses in America. Some thirty-five years later, there were only about half as many.

Mechanized tractors, plows, and harvesters took over much of the hard farm labor. They made farming much more productive. The mechanical reaper is a good example. With it, two workers could cut fourteen times as much wheat as before.

American farmers supplied the nation with more than just crops. Their cows produced millions of gallons of milk. And the sheep, hogs, and cattle that they raised helped make the United States the best-fed nation in the world.

Most of the country's beef, however, was provided by a particular group of workers in the West — the American cowboys. Cowboys have been celebrated in songs, stories, and films. They rank among the most romantic figures in all of American history. What is often overlooked, however, is that cowboys (and cowgirls) were important agricultural workers. Aside from their adventures and heroics, they were responsible for raising, caring for, and driving to market the huge herds of cattle that supplied the nation with so much of its meat.

Cowboys did not fence in their cattle. Instead they allowed them to graze freely on government-owned grasslands. Every spring, cowboy outfits got together for a spring "roundup." There were two purposes to this roundup. One was to move the cattle northward. The other was to mark calves that had been born that year with the brand of the owner. In the following account a cowboy describes one of these roundups.

In His Own Words:
A COWBOY

THE PURPOSE of pushing all the cattle as far northward as possible is to keep them on the proper range. Cattle never move north on their own. They seldom move east or west. Every storm, coming as they do from the north, drives the cattle to the south. If we did not drive them northward yearly then all of the cattle of the entire Western country would in time pack themselves into southern Texas.

"It looks like it might be a bad night," says the range boss. "You better saddle your night ponies and be ready to go on the herd at any moment." Two hours go by. Suddenly a flash of lightning blazes in the northwest and soon a dull rumble of thunder follows.

All hands are roused out. Grumbling, we ride out to the herd. A stampede must be avoided. The riders go circling around the herd. They accompany their efforts with whistle, song, and shout. Meanwhile the rain begins. The lightning grows brighter. The thunder has grown into a never-ending roar and the frightened herd with heads upraised and eyes glaring push about, ready to stampede. This would mean serious business, this turning $100,000 worth of cattle loose in pitch darkness, breaking their legs and necks over cliffs and rocks. So the boys crowd upon the herd, still circling it, riding harder and singing louder than ever.

At last morning breaks and the storm dies away. The herd is again composed and we sleepily gather for breakfast.

Adapted from *Trailing the Cowboy: His Life and Lore as Told by Frontier Journalists*, by Clifford P. Westermeier, The Caxton Printers, Ltd., Caldwell, Idaho, 1955. (The cowboy in this account was part of a roundup that took place in 1881.)

Mining

THE UNITED STATES has always been blessed with a great number of natural resources. Many of these resources, such as coal, iron ore, copper, and other minerals, lie under the ground. They need to be dug out, or mined, in order to be put into use.

Coal, for example, has always been an extremely important resource in the production of heat and power. Today most houses and businesses are heated by oil, gas, or electricity. But in the late 1800s and well into the 1900s, most people used coal to heat their homes, and coal is still used as a source of power in many of the nation's largest industries.

The miners who worked miles beneath the ground digging out the coal and other minerals led extremely difficult lives. Working conditions were horrible and terribly dangerous. Thousands of miners lost their lives each year in tragic mine accidents.

Nonetheless, in the year 1890 alone, almost a half million Americans were employed in the nation's mines—and this work force included a great many children, forced into a life of mining by families who needed every dollar in order to survive.

Miners supplied the coal that kept the nation's industries going. Their work helped make the United States the leading industrial nation in the world. Yet for the miners themselves there was little reward. The dangers were great, and since picks, shovels, and sledgehammers were the main tools of the trade, the work was very hard.

From two to three thousand workers were killed in mine accidents every year. Thousands more were seriously injured. In order to combat this, miners trained in first aid began to organize themselves into lifesaving crews. They used the latest equipment available.

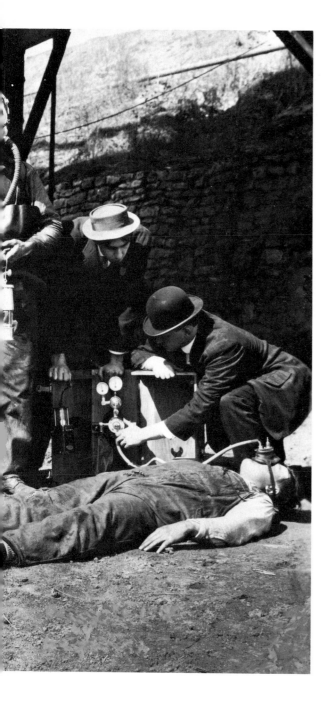

In His Own Words:
A MINER

I AM THIRTY-FIVE YEARS OLD, married, and the father of four children. I have worked in the coal region all my life. Twenty-three of these years have been spent in and around the mines. My father was a miner. He died ten years ago from "miner's asthma."

Three of my brothers are miners. None of us had any chance to get an education. We were sent to school (such a school as there was in those days) until we were about twelve. Then we were put into the mines. There were five of us boys. One lies in the cemetery. Fifty tons of top rock dropped on him.

Day in and day out, from Monday morning to Saturday evening, between the rising and the setting of the sun, I am in the underground workings of the coal mines. From the seams water trickles into the ditches along the gangways. If not water, it is the gas which hurls us to eternity. We get old quickly. Powder, smoke, bad air—all combine to bring furrows to our faces and asthma to our lungs.

Our condition can be no worse. It might and must be better. The luxuries of the rich we do not ask. We do want butter for our bread and meat for our soup. We do not want silk and laces for our wives and daughters. But we want to earn enough to buy them a simple clean dress once in a while. Our boys are not expecting automobiles. But they want their fathers to earn enough to keep them at school until they have a reasonably fair education.

Adapted from an article in *The Independent*, 1902. (The miner in this account was employed in a mine in Pennsylvania.)

One of the most tragic features of mining was the number of children who were used in the work. Boys, twelve years and under, sat on crude benches for ten or twelve hours every day as lumps of coal passed down a chute at their feet. Called breaker boys, the youngsters would pick out pieces of slate that had become mixed in with the coal.

Not all mining was done underground. Then, as now, strip-mining and open-pit mining operations were also carried on. In open-pit or strip-mining, workers do not go beneath the ground. Rather, huge chunks of earth are stripped away. Then the mineral being mined—copper, for example— is separated from the earth. The coming of huge machinery made open-pit and strip-mining more profitable. The photograph shows an open-pit copper mine in New Mexico.

The Age of Sailing Ships

THE UNITED STATES has always been linked closely to the sea. The settlers in the original colonies huddled close to the eastern seaboard, and depended upon the sea not only as a link to European countries but also as an important means of livelihood.   ·

As the nation grew, many Americans earned their living at jobs relating to the sea. In the age of sailing vessels there were shipbuilders, sea captains, sailors, sailmakers, dockworkers, barrelmakers, harbor pilots, and thousands of other workers who earned their living either by servicing ships or by sailing on them. By the middle of the 1800s, America was one of the greatest seafaring nations in the world.

To many people, there was nothing more beautiful than a clipper or a sloop or a packet or even a fishing schooner with its sails full-out, billowing in the wind. It took great skill to build and to sail these vessels. And shipbuilders, owners, and sailors took great pride in their ships.

American sailing vessels could be found in ports around the world. And in a day when there were no airplanes and the railroad was in its infancy, most goods within the United States were shipped by sea from one port to another. Some of the sailing vessels were of great size and could carry huge loads of products such as lumber and coal.

Thousands of Americans earned their living in shipyards where the sailing vessels were built and launched. It took a large number of skilled workers to build a huge sailing ship. The workers were divided into crews, each with its particular task. Besides gangs of carpenters, there were crews with names like joiners, dubbers, riggers, and scrapers.

This striking photograph shows the vessel *John J. Christopher* in a stage of building known as "inframe." The inside and outside of the huge timbers that make up the frame have been smoothed and shaped by workers called dubbers. The planking that runs across the top of the hull is either hard pine or oak. American loggers were kept busy supplying the nation's shipyards with timber for masts, frames, decking, and all the other parts of the hundreds of sailing vessels that were built each year.

Shipbuilders took great pride in their work. Each was an artist at his craft. And in an age when great attention was paid to detail, American ships could stand proudly alongside those of any other nation.

The masts of the tall ships filled the harbors of American ports around the country. The busy ports were like cities in themselves. There were sailmakers', carpenters', and blacksmiths' shops. There also were the rope-walks, where the miles of rope used on sailing vessels were made. In other shops men called coopers made the barrels used to carry cargo, while crafts-men known as chandlers made the millions of candles used every year at sea. And along the wharves were the many ships' supply stores and build-ings where the shipping merchants had their offices.

Sailing vessels were often the victims of violent storms and unfamiliar seas. Hundreds of wrecks occurred each year and countless sailors lost their lives. The man standing next to the lifeboat was a member of a United States Lifesaving Service team. The Lifesaving Service had stations along both the Atlantic and Pacific coasts. They performed heroic deeds and saved many lives. The crew of this vessel were very lucky. Their ship was driven aground in a huge storm but remained upright without loss of life.

The United States has always had two great frontiers. One has been the land frontier, which was pushed farther and farther westward until pioneers settled all the land from coast to coast. The other frontier has been the sea. This is the frontier that American fishermen have faced as they have pushed their vessels far out into the oceans.

Fish has always been an important food. Even before European nations settled America, they sent ships to the rich fishing grounds of the New World. Colonial Americans depended on their fishermen for much of their food.

One of the richest of all the world's fishing grounds lies off the eastern coast of the United States, from Long Island to Newfoundland. In the late 1800s, New England fishermen sailed their fishing schooners to these waters. They netted huge quantities of haddock, mackerel, halibut, and cod. Fishing ports like Gloucester and Boston became famous as American fishermen helped fill tables all over the world with their catch.

A big halibut is hoisted onto the dock. Halibut vessels fished the waters off Newfoundland, Greenland, and Iceland. It was hard work. The men fished in water over two hundred fathoms deep where ice floes were always a danger. It took great skill to catch these fish and only the best fishermen were employed in the halibut fishery.

The photograph shows T Wharf in Boston in 1902. At the turn of the
century Boston was the leading fresh-fish market in the nation. All of the
ships tied up to the wharf are fishing schooners.

In His Own Words:
A FIFTEEN-YEAR-OLD FISHERMAN

WE LEFT WATER COVE for the Sau' Sau' West Grounds off Monhegan Island in the *Eva and Mildred* with a crew of ten fishermen and a cook. Father was the skipper. He made it just as tough for me as he could and I was called on to do everything the older men did. We had breakfast before daylight. Then we went off in the small boats to set the nets. We were picked up for lunch. Then we went back to haul the nets in.

Two or three miles of nets with a good catch of fish in it comes in hard for a fifteen-year-old boy. Each man was back on board with his catch by the middle of the afternoon. We had supper, and then dressed the fish. When that was done we baited the nets for the next day. With a full load we made a twenty-four-hour run to T Wharf in Boston, sold our catch and shared $27.10 apiece. That was big money in them times for four days of fishin'. When everything was shipshape on board, the men invited me to go uptown with 'em to a beer parlor.

With money in my pocket and a bunch of friends I never felt bigger in my life and I was set for the next trip.

Adapted from an unpublished diary, 1897. (The boy who wrote the diary later became the owner of his own fishing vessel.)

Not all the sailing ships used in fishing were schooners. Some were smaller, one-masted vessels called sloops. These ships were used in going after large fish like swordfish.

A man known as a striker stood in what was called the pulpit of the ship, harpoon in hand. The harpoon was attached by rope to a barrel in the sloop. When the fish was harpooned the barrel was thrown overboard. The men then waited until the fish exhausted itself trying to get away. Then they would get into the dory that was towed in back of the sloop. From the dory they would kill the swordfish and haul it aboard.

Fishing did not end with the catch. Once the fish were brought to the home port they had to be unloaded. Then they were cleaned, cut up, packed into barrels of ice, and shipped to market.

The Age of Steamships

B Y THE END of the 1800s, great changes were taking place in the way people earned their living from the sea. Steam-powered vessels were replacing wind-driven ships. Sailing vessels depended on wind, currents, and tide. Steamships, on the other hand, could go where they pleased, when they pleased.

Steam engines could drive the biggest of ships. More passengers and cargo could be carried by sea than ever before. Gradually many of those who worked on sailing vessels switched over to steamships. And workers who had earned their living by servicing sailing ships quickly learned how to service the new steam-driven vessels.

Steamships carried travelers to places around the globe. They made regular runs on American rivers and lakes and hauled huge loads of cargo across the ocean and from one American port to another. Fishing, too, was affected by the perfection of the steam engine. Heavier steam-driven vessels made it possible for fishermen to go farther out after their catch. They could haul more net and store more fish than ever before.

A day's outing on a steamboat became one of America's favorite pastimes. Every major river and lake had ships that made regular runs from one city or town to another. Family outings by sea became a popular event.

All along both the East and West coasts large steamship lines were established. Like the automobile, the train, and the airplane, steamships shrank distances. They helped make Americans the most mobile people in the world.

"Steamboat a-comin!" This magic cry was heard throughout America. And even the sleepiest of towns came alive as the vessels packed with passengers and freight came into view.

In His Own Words:
MARK TWAIN DESCRIBES THE ARRIVAL OF A STEAMBOAT

A FILM of dark smoke appears. A teamster lifts up the cry, "s-t-e-a-m-boat a comin'!" The town drunkard stirs, the clerks wake up and a furious clatter of wagons follows. In a twinkling the dead town is alive and moving. Wagons, carts, men, boys all go hurrying to a common center, the wharf.

The steamboat is long and sharp and trim and pretty. She has two tall, fancy-topped chimneys and a fanciful pilothouse all glass and "gingerbread." The paddle-boxes are gorgeous with a picture above the ship's name. The decks are fenced with clean white railings.

The upper decks are black with passengers. The captain stands by the big bell, calm and imposing, the envy of all. The crew are grouped on the forecastle. The broad stage is run far out over the port bow. An envied deck hand stands on the end of it with a coil of rope. The captain lifts his hand, a bell rings, and the wheels stop. Then they turn back, churning the water to foam, and the steamer is at rest.

Then such a scramble as there is to get aboard, and to get ashore, and to take in freight, and to discharge freight, all at once and the same time. Ten minutes later the steamer is underway again. After ten more minutes the town is dead and the town drunkard is asleep once more.

Adapted from *Life on the Mississippi* by Samuel Clemens, 1883. (Samuel Clemens is better known by his pen name, Mark Twain. The town in this account was Twain's boyhood home, Hannibal, Missouri.)

There were almost as many different kinds of steamships as there were different kinds of sailing vessels. Many of the early ships had huge paddle wheels on either the side or the rear.

These paddle wheelers were a common sight on one of the world's great waterways—the Mississippi River. Thousands of tons of goods each year were carried up and down the Mississippi. All along the river, workers toiled at loading and unloading the vessels.

On the Move

From Horse and Wagon to Airplane

THE LATE 1800s and early 1900s are sometimes known as the Era of the Great Transportation Revolution. It was a period in which such important inventions as the trolley, the train, the automobile, and the airplane were perfected. Nothing in our history, before or since, has changed life in America as much as did this transportation revolution.

Hundreds of thousands of jobs were created by these new means of travel. In 1890 alone, for example, more than half a million men and women worked for American railroads. Trolley lines, which sprang up in cities and towns all over the United States, employed many others. Automobiles and airplanes were still in their infancy, but they, too, were creating new forms of travel and whole new types of employment.

Even with these new inventions, however, it was still a time when horses and wagons were as common a sight as cars and trucks today. Thousands of people earned their living by driving these horse-drawn wagons. They sold all kinds of products from house to house. And until motortrucks were perfected later in the 1900s, horses and wagons were still the chief way that goods and services were delivered directly to the customer.

Horse and wagon, trolley, train, automobile, airplane—all were important to the transportation revolution. All were vital avenues of work for Americans "on the move."

Today most of us buy our milk at grocery stores or supermarkets. In the late 1800s, however, milk sellers sold their products from door to door. Customers had their own bottles or jugs. They would have them filled from the huge cans in the milk cart.

In His Own Words:
A TEAMSTER

I WAS BORN in Philadelphia on October 5, 1888, but came to San Francisco as a baby. My father was a teamster. There were seven children in the family, four boys and three girls. The boys all became teamsters. I went to work at around age fourteen.

As a teamster, my hours of work were from sunup to sundown. It was a seven day a week job. Monday through Saturday was actually the work week. On Sunday it would be necessary for us to go to the barn to feed, water, and brush the horses and clean the harnesses.

My duties were those of the average teamster. I picked up goods and delivered them to and from the San Francisco docks. Although our wages were not high by today's comparisons, the dollar of that day was worth one hundred cents. For instance, hamburger could be purchased for about thirteen cents a pound. Coffee was about fifteen cents per pound. Sugar was twenty pounds for one dollar and butter was thirty cents per pound. The usual teamster's home was an ordinary, typical San Francisco flat with two bedrooms, kitchen, dining room, sitting room or "parlor." The rent was generally about $18 a month.

About 1917 the automotive trucks began to replace horse-drawn vehicles. The average teamster certainly did not welcome the coming of the motor truck. There was, however, a gradual change among teamsters. Soon they became able to handle various motor trucks. Driving motor trucks did reduce our work week, because there was no need to go to the barns on Sunday to take care of the horses as we had to do before.

Adapted from *Teamster Life in San Francisco Before World War I*, Oral History Project, University of California, 1958.

During this period, peddlers of every type had regular routes through city, town, and country. There was no such thing as a supermarket. There were small grocery stores, but people relied heavily on those who drove meat wagons, fish wagons, vegetable wagons, and bakery wagons. Meat peddlers, for example, would show their products to the customer and then custom-cut an order on the spot. There were many other types of peddlers as well. They sold everything from brooms and mops to sewing machines.

One of the most common sights in city and town was the iceman and his wagon. There were no refrigerators. Food was kept cold in an insulated "icebox." Children who gathered around the ice wagon were often there for a very special reason. They waited hopefully for permission to "snitch" some of the cool ice to lick on a hot afternoon.

The photograph shows an electric trolley that ran through the streets of Washington, D.C., in the 1890s. The driver and his two fellow employees were but three of thousands of people who were employed by the trolley systems that sprang up throughout the nation. Electric trolleys made it possible for people to move about in growing cities more easily than they ever had before. Late in the 1890s, interurban trolley systems were established. These trolleys connected cities up to fifty miles apart. They enabled people to travel to beaches, amusement parks, and mountain resorts.

In His Own Words:

ADVICE FROM A VETERAN TROLLEY WORKER

DO NOT lose your temper! Many a motorman has lost his position because of a quick temper. I remember a motorman who was always ill-tempered. The minute he got his hands on the controls, he was angry at everything and everyone. The conducter was too slow, the passengers were too slow, or too many people were riding. I personally know of one accident he was entirely to blame for because of his temper.

Do not forget your personal appearance. Nothing gives a motorman a better stand in the public eye than to be clean and neatly dressed. If there is anything that disgusts me, it is to sit behind a motorman and gaze on a neck so dirty that you could raise a crop of potatoes on it.

Adapted from "Advice to Motormen," published in a company pamphlet by the Chicago Trolley Company in 1904.

In 1830 the United States had only twenty-three miles of railroads. By 1870 there were more than fifty thousand miles of track. Railroads linked American cities together and speeded settlement of the West. Wherever trains ran, people could settle, raise crops and cattle, and then ship these goods to market by train.

Thousands of workers labored at laying the tracks and building the bridges that allowed trains to go almost anywhere. By 1869, a railroad line ran all the way across the country, connecting East with West.

It took all kinds of workers to keep the growing railroads in operation. There were tracklayers, yard crews, ticket sellers, conductors, engineers, flagmen, and porters—to name but a few. And there were also the skilled workers who built the beautiful and powerful engines that pulled the trains across America.

Today, in an age when most people travel by automobile or airplane, it is easy to lose sight of the fact that there was a time when trains were the most popular form of transportation in America.

Passenger trains could be very elegant. This was particularly true of dining cars. Great attention was paid to every detail, from the lighting fixtures to the beautiful wood paneling. And the food was well served and delicious.

Freight trains were far from elegant, but they were extremely important to the railroads and to the nation as a whole. All kinds of goods were carried, and railroads and industry were closely linked together. Freight trains also took farmers' and ranchers' goods to market. The photograph shows a fifty-car cattle train on its way through Nevada to the Chicago stockyards.

In the early 1900s, millions of Americans traveled by train. In the account that follows, a thirteen-year-old girl describes her first trip to a railroad station.

In Her Own Words:
AT THE TRAIN STATION

AT LAST the day came. We woke early, got into our best clothes, and were at the station by eight o'clock. Never had I seen such a busy place. Trains were pulling in and pulling out. Bells seemed to be clanging from everywhere. A man with a very loud voice announced each train as it came in or left the station. He spoke so quickly I could not understand much of what he was saying.

There were people everywhere. Porters heaped baggage in huge piles on large, flat carts. I was sure we would never see ours again. Men and young boys sold everything from newspapers to combs to fried dough. The fried dough smelled delicious, but father said we would be eating on the train.

Mother kept telling me to stay inside the station and not go near the tracks. Once I poked my head outside the doors. Loud noises and huge billows of steam were coming from underneath the trains. There were railroad workers everywhere. Some had very fancy suits and hats with badges on them. Others were in coveralls. They carried lunch pails and tools with them. They all looked very important.

Finally father grabbed my hand and said that our train was here. Before I really knew what was happening I was in my seat. Then there was a huge hiss of steam, a cry of "B-o-a-r-d!" and we were underway.

Adapted from an unpublished manuscript, by Laura Corbin, 1902.

No single invention has changed American life more than the automobile. By 1910 there were sixty-nine automobile companies in the United States. In the next twenty years, the Ford Motor Company alone had made twenty million cars. This was enough automobiles to circle the world bumper to bumper. The automobile craze that captured America created countless new jobs. Thousands of men and women went to work in the factories where the cars were made. Others found jobs in industries that made products like automobile tires, seat cushions, lights, gasoline, and oil.

Thousands of miles of roads were built to handle the new auto traffic. And in city and country, the automobile was used as a working machine to do all sorts of things. In cities like New York, for example, sight-seeing buses made their appearance. Those who drove them had to be skilled drivers as they made their way through city streets crowded with people, horses, carts, trolleys, and a rapidly growing number of automobiles. In the country the automobile began to be used in one of America's oldest occupations—the delivery of mail.

The photograph above shows Helen Simpson. She was one of America's first woman pilots. As aviation grew, people took jobs as pilots, mechanics, stewardesses, flight schedulers, ticket sellers, baggage handlers, and airmail carriers. By 1920 there were regularly scheduled air-passenger lines in the United States, and a coast-to-coast airmail route.

From the beginning, the air industry attracted people in search of thrills and adventure. Some men and women even earned a living by performing dangerous stunts while hundreds of feet over the earth.

The Factories

THE LATE 1800s and early 1900s were truly remarkable years. Inventions and scientific discoveries led to both the transportation and the industrial revolutions. People could move about in machines never dreamed of by their grandparents. And other kinds of machines could manufacture goods faster and in greater numbers than was ever thought possible.

The buildings that housed the manufacturing machines were called factories. Tens of thousands of people went to work in these factories. They made hard goods like sewing machines, farm machinery, and baby carriages. They worked on soft goods such as clothing of all kinds and paper products.

The factories, for the most part, were not pleasant places in which to work. They were steaming hot in the summer and frigid in the winter. They were often overcrowded and the work around the machines was dangerous. Nonetheless, people stood in line to get jobs in factories. Many of the people who worked there had come to America from European countries. Many young people, tired of farm work, moved to the city and worked in the mills. And all over America a great many women left their traditional jobs as homemakers and joined the ranks of factory workers.

There were many reasons why so many women went to work in the factories. Many simply needed the money. Others were tired of being tied down to the home. They saw the factories as a way of getting out on their own. Some industries had almost all women workers.

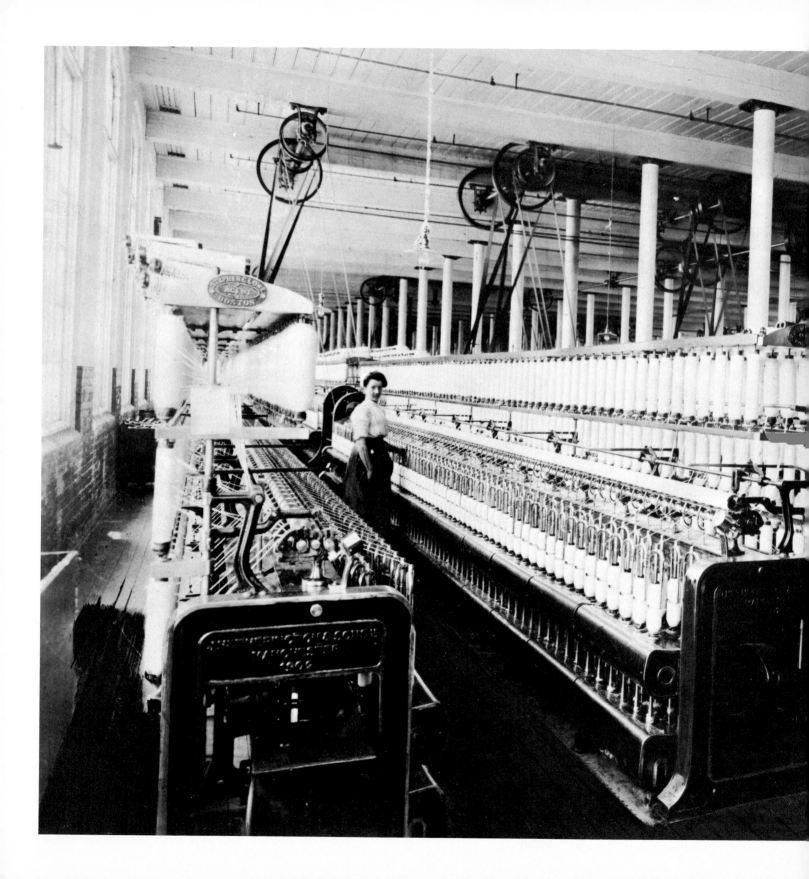

Sadie Frowne was a young woman who came from Poland to America. At the age of seventeen she went to work in a shirt factory in New York. In the following account she describes her work.

In Her Own Words:
A FACTORY WORKER

I WENT to work in what is called a factory. I made shirts by machine. I was new at the work and the boss scolded me a great deal.

The factory is in the third floor of a brick building. It is twenty feet long and fourteen feet wide. There are fourteen machines in it. I get up at half past five every morning. I have a cup of coffee, a bit of bread and then go to work. Often I get to the factory at six o'clock.

The machines go like mad all day. Sometimes in my haste I get my finger caught and the needle goes right through it. It goes so quick that it does not hurt much. I bind the finger up with a piece of cotton and go on working. We all have accidents like that.

While we work the boss walks around checking the finished shirts. He makes us do them over again if they are not right. But I am getting good at the work. By next year I will be making seven dollars a week. The machines are run by foot power. At the end of the day I feel so weak that I could just lie down and sleep.

But I am going back to night school again this winter. Plenty of my friends go there. Like me, they did not have a chance to learn anything in the old country. It is good to have an education. It makes you feel higher.

Adapted from "The Story of a Sweatshop Girl," *The Independent,* 1902.

The industrial revolution brought with it many changes in the way goods were made. One of the most important was the assembly-line process. Before assembly lines were used, one worker made an entire product. For example, in a gun factory a worker would make each part of the gun and then put the whole weapon together. This took quite a long time.

In an assembly line, workers stand along a moving belt. The product being made moves along the belt and each worker performs one task in the manufacturing process as the product passes by. By the time the product gets to the end of the line it is finished.

Assembly lines produced goods faster than ever before. Almost every industry began using them and in the early 1900s Henry Ford introduced them into his automobile factory. Ford studied and improved the assembly-line system so well that by 1925 his factories were producing a car a minute.

Construction

IN THE YEAR 1790 less than 3 percent of all Americans lived in cities. By 1900 more than 31 percent were city dwellers. The industrial revolution changed more than just how Americans worked. It changed how and where they lived as well.

The rapid growth of American cities brought a huge building boom to the nation. By 1900 more than a million people were working at one kind of building job or another. There were about 750,000 carpenters alone.

As people poured into the cities, more and more houses and office buildings were needed. Carpenters and construction workers of all types were kept busy from sunup to sundown. And it was not only in the cities that the building boom was on. In small towns all over America, stores and houses were being built. And bricklayers, plasterers, roofers, and cabinetmakers, as well as carpenters, found themselves in great demand.

One of the most important products of the industrial revolution was steel. Steel made the growth of cities possible. Steel cables were used for bridges. Steel was strong enough to support buildings so tall that people called them skyscrapers. In places like New York, Chicago, and St. Louis, men worked on steel beams high above the city, putting the skyscrapers together.

As cities grew, more and more services were needed. Many of these services grew out of inventions of the time. Wires were strung for electrical and telephone service. Bridges and tunnels were built. And miles of trolley tracks were laid.

New inventions kept appearing to help construction workers with their task. This new steam-operated crane appeared about the year 1880. The umbrella kept the operator out of the sun. But obviously the crane could go only where there were railroad tracks to hold it.

In Her Own Words:

DAUGHTER OF A CONSTRUCTION COMPANY OWNER

MY FATHER was the best stone mason and bricklayer in the town. He was even better than the man who had taught him his trade. Father would often take us to the houses he was building. He would take us also to the bridges that were under construction. My youngest sister and I were always amazed by it all.

Dad would allow us to climb in and about the houses. He would show us how to mix the mortar and handle the trowel. I remember how he used to love his tools. He wouldn't let anyone borrow them.

At an early age we acquired a deep respect for working people. We were part of them. We were taught to particularly respect the people who worked for Dad. This was true of the laborers as well as the mechanics.

Our house was simply but tastefully furnished. We had a good piano. This was because mother thought there should be entertainment in the house. Many colored families had big, expensive houses. But we were the only colored children who belonged to the private library. There was no public library and mother had to pay for the cards. Each of us had a card of our own. As to politics, father thought a man was a good candidate if he understood the working people.

Adapted from *The Negro Family in the United States*, by E. Franklin Frazier, Dryden Press, 1948.

Once roads, streets, and trolley tracks were constructed, they had to be kept open and in good repair. In both the city and the country people earned their living by working on roads and streets. Winter posed particular problems to these workers. And snow was handled differently in the country than it was in the city.

Child Labor

THE LATE 1800s and early 1900s were exciting years for millions of Americans. The nation's economy was on the rise and there were many good things to be bought and enjoyed. The growing cities, for example, became centers of entertainment where people could find stores, restaurants, theaters, dance halls, and sporting events. And many people had the money to enjoy all these pleasures.

This was not true of all Americans, however. Many people, particularly the tens of thousands of immigrants who poured into the nation from all over the world during that period, had little money. Many were so desperate that they were forced to send their children to work at very early ages.

Therefore, it was not unusual to find children from eight to twelve years old working all day long in all kinds of jobs. They worked in factories, on the streets, in the mines, and in countless other places. There was little time for play and less time for education. Many of the child workers never set foot inside a schoolroom.

As the years went on, private citizens and public officials began to work toward bringing about reforms that would make the hiring of children illegal. One of these reformers was a man named Louis Hine.

Hine was an important photographer who devoted his life to a crusade against child labor. He took thousands of pictures of young children at work. His photographs were then presented to government agencies that were studying working conditions in America.

Louis Hine's pictures did much to bring about the reforms that made child labor illegal. The following pages contain some of the photographs he took and used in his important crusade.

Public Servants

THOSE PEOPLE who work for the good of others are, of course, terribly important in every society. Policemen, firemen, nurses, and teachers, for example, provide services that no modern community can do without.

American cities grew rapidly during the late 1800s and early 1900s. One reason for this was the large number of immigrants who made the cities their new home. Another was that the factories attracted workers to the cities where they were located. As the cities grew, more and more policemen were needed to keep order. Unfortunately, there were a great number of fires, especially since so many of the buildings were made of wood. Large fire departments had to be kept.

Health care was particularly needed. Sickness spread rapidly in the crowded areas and many people could not afford private medical care. Nurses and doctors who were employed by cities worked long hours to maintain the public health.

And then, as now, education was extremely important to most people. Many of the immigrants, for example, realized that if their children were going to succeed in their new land they would need a proper education. Teachers were important members of every community. In 1900, almost half a million Americans, most of them women, earned their living as teachers.

In many cities places called settlement houses were set up. There immigrant men and women could learn to speak and write English. People with personal problems could go to the neighborhood settlement house for help.

Most settlement houses had their own staff of nurses. This nurse was on her rounds to visit the sick. She took a route familiar to many early city dwellers—over the tenement rooftops.

Then, as now, policemen were a common sight in American cities and towns. However, they did dress differently then and they certainly had different methods of moving about.

The policemen lined up for their morning instructions were, believe it or not, the full White House police force assigned to protect President Theodore Roosevelt. There was no Secret Service then and Presidents and their families moved about much more freely than they do today.

In His Own Words:
A FIREMAN

I HAD ALWAYS WANTED to be a fireman. When I was a youngster I would chase the engine to every fire in the neighborhood.

When I first joined the department all of the fire companies in town were privately owned. We got paid according to how many fires we put out. You can imagine what would happen when the fire bell rang. Every company in the area would race around looking for the fire. Sometimes there were actually fist fights over which company was the first to set up its hoses. Meanwhile the fire would burn on.

I've been a fireman now for some twenty-two years. We've had some really bad fires in this city. I'm not sure that people understand how much we risk for them but if they could follow us around for a few days they'd find out. I've lost two of my best friends in the past three years. One was trapped inside a building. The other fell off our engine on the way to a fire.

Since my wife died I've been living at the firehouse. Actually it's good for the company because it means there's someone here day and night. We have an engine, a pumper, and two ladder teams. When we're not at a fire we spend most of our time shining the equipment and caring for the horses. Last year we won the prize for best appearance by a fire team.

Adapted from an unpublished manuscript, by Walter G. Davis, written in 1894. (Mr. Davis was a fireman in Baltimore, Maryland.)

Schools in those days looked different from the average school today. In most cities and towns, students sat on wooden benches. The schoolroom was heated by a large potbellied stove in the middle of the room. In the winter the teacher had to be an excellent fire maker as well as instructor.

In farm and frontier country, schools were even more rustic. Most had only one room and students of all grades would attend class together. Communities in the farm and frontier areas often did not have enough money to pay teachers in cash. Instead, parents would take turns feeding the teachers, giving them a place to stay, and providing them with farm products like eggs and milk.

Private Servants

IN THE LATE 1800s and early 1900s the gap between the rich and the poor was very great. The majority of Americans, however, fell somewhere in between as far as income and living styles were concerned. There were no income taxes then, and there were many people in America who could afford great luxuries. These luxuries included household servants.

Some of the rich were very rich indeed. One man, William Vanderbilt, for example, had a mansion with 110 rooms. There were 45 bathrooms and a garage ready to hold 100 automobiles. He had other houses as well and at any one time he employed almost 500 servants.

There were not many William Vanderbilts, it is true. However, in those days one did not have to be very rich to have servants, since there were so many poor people who were willing to work for very little. Thus in these years hundreds of thousands of people earned their living as private servants. In fact, next to farming, more Americans were employed as household servants in 1900 than in any other job! Almost one and a half million women alone were engaged in some kind of household service.

Household servants included cooks, maids, butlers, caretakers, gardeners, stable keepers, liverymen, and countless others. Many people were attracted to this type of work because good food, a good place to live, pleasant surroundings, and at least one day off a week were usually included in the working conditions.

Liverymen were a common sight at the homes of the very rich. They cared for and drove the elegant carriages that were part of the estate. At parties the liverymen would dress in elegant outfits and would line up along the driveway, greeting the guests as they arrived.

Many women earned their living at this time by living in people's homes and caring for their children. There was an added bonus to this job. When the parents traveled or went to their seaside or mountain homes, those who cared for the children got to go with them.

Meals were often very formal affairs in the homes of the wealthy. Cooks, butlers, table maids—many servants could be involved in one meal.

In Her Own Words:
A SERVANT

AT FIRST I could not believe what the lady had said to me.

  "Seven dollars a week and room and board. Do you mean it?"

  "Of course, and Saturday and Sunday for your own."

  "And I can have a nice room in a first-class house? Why, of course I'll take it."

Oh how good it was. And what a delight to use the bath. A lovely parlor and a piano were at my service.

The work is not the most pleasant in the world, but I can recommend it to other unskilled hands. I do not enjoy washing clothes, but most of my work is ironing. When I was keeping house for myself I never had time to get any one task done well, but here I have time to do every piece perfectly.

Every Sunday I have an invitation to go somewhere. This summer I have been to weekend parties at the shore. I have both time and money for trolley rides and the theatre. The hard work makes muscle and digests food, and a pleasant Saturday and Sunday are always ahead of me.

Adapted from an article in *The Independent*, 1904.

Store Owners and Store Workers

THE UNITED STATES has always been a nation of storekeepers. In the earliest days many people had stores in their homes. They sold goods like cloth and yarn from which people could make their own finished products. The industrial revolution not only provided the nation with thousands of new manufactured items, but it enabled factories to turn out ready-to-buy finished goods. More stores than ever before were needed to sell this new merchandise.

Almost every new product created businesses related to it. For example, the making of automobiles brought about car agencies, tire stores, and gas stations. With so many goods to sell, whole new types of stores were created. Large department stores where all kinds of items were sold under one roof were opened. Huge mail-order houses like Sears, Roebuck also appeared. Now people in even the most remote areas could buy the latest products.

Store owners and store workers provided not only goods but services. Barbershops and beauty shops, repair stores of all kinds, and real-estate offices could be found in every city and town. And there was always the soda shop, the meat market, and the local restaurant, where people could spend their money and pass the time of day.

The soda shop was the favorite gathering place for millions of Americans, young and old. Most shop owners took great pride in the appearance of their stores. This could be seen in every detail, from the polished counters and showcases to the store decorations.

Then, as now, many kinds of repair services were provided by American stores. Many of those who provided these services were highly skilled. They had to be to keep up with all the new products and inventions.

Almost every city and town of any size had its barbershop. There, as in other stores, great attention was paid to detail. Bottles were perfectly arranged. Every towel was in its place. And store owners expected their workers to be as neat in their appearance and in their work as were their surroundings.

In His Own Words:
A RESTAURANT OWNER

I WAS FIFTEEN years old when I first started to work in res-taurants. The place would open for breakfast at six so I had to be there at 5:30. Many a morning I made the coffee, got out the bread and rolls and set up the counter while still half asleep.

The first restaurant I worked in was near the wharves. It attracted a large, noisy crowd. By six-thirty the place would be filled with dock workers and teamsters demanding this and in-sisting on that. I think it was the only chance they got to order other people around. But they were really good-natured at heart. After I was there for a while they stopped playing jokes on me and we got along O.K.

Prices then were much lower than now. I remember we sold a breakfast of ham, eggs, potatoes, roll, and coffee for ten cents. Pie was three cents a slice and you got a big bowl of oatmeal for two cents.

This is the second restaurant I've owned. The railroad ran track right where I had my first one. I like the restaurant busi-ness. I like talking and kidding around with people. Although some customers can be very nasty. You can never please them. They don't seem to realize that you're a human being, too.

It's not an easy business. There's long hours and seven days a week. And things go wrong. Last month the factory went on strike and a lot of my food went bad before I could use it. But I'll always be a restaurant man. It's all I know.

Adapted from an unpublished manuscript by Francis R. Logan, written in 1901. (Mr. Logan's restaurant was in St. Louis, Missouri.)

It was an age when customers expected that the products sold them would work as advertised. Store owners knew most of their customers personally. This jeweler, for example, made sure that every watch was working as well as possible. His business depended upon it.

Thousands of people went to work in the new department stores. They sold everything from yard goods to fishing rods to bicycles. For the first time, shoppers could make many of their purchases under one roof.

American businessmen have always been ready to take advantage of any business opportunities presented them. As soon as frontier areas were settled, for example, businessmen set up stores of all kinds to serve customers.

Even the goldfields of the Far West were not too far away to attract store owners. Throughout the late 1800s accounts of gold strikes were reported in various areas of the West Coast. Thousands of people flocked to these lands in search of instant wealth. About the only ones who made any money were the enterprising individuals who carted goods across the country, set up crude stores, and sold pick handles for ten dollars apiece and eggs at two dollars each.

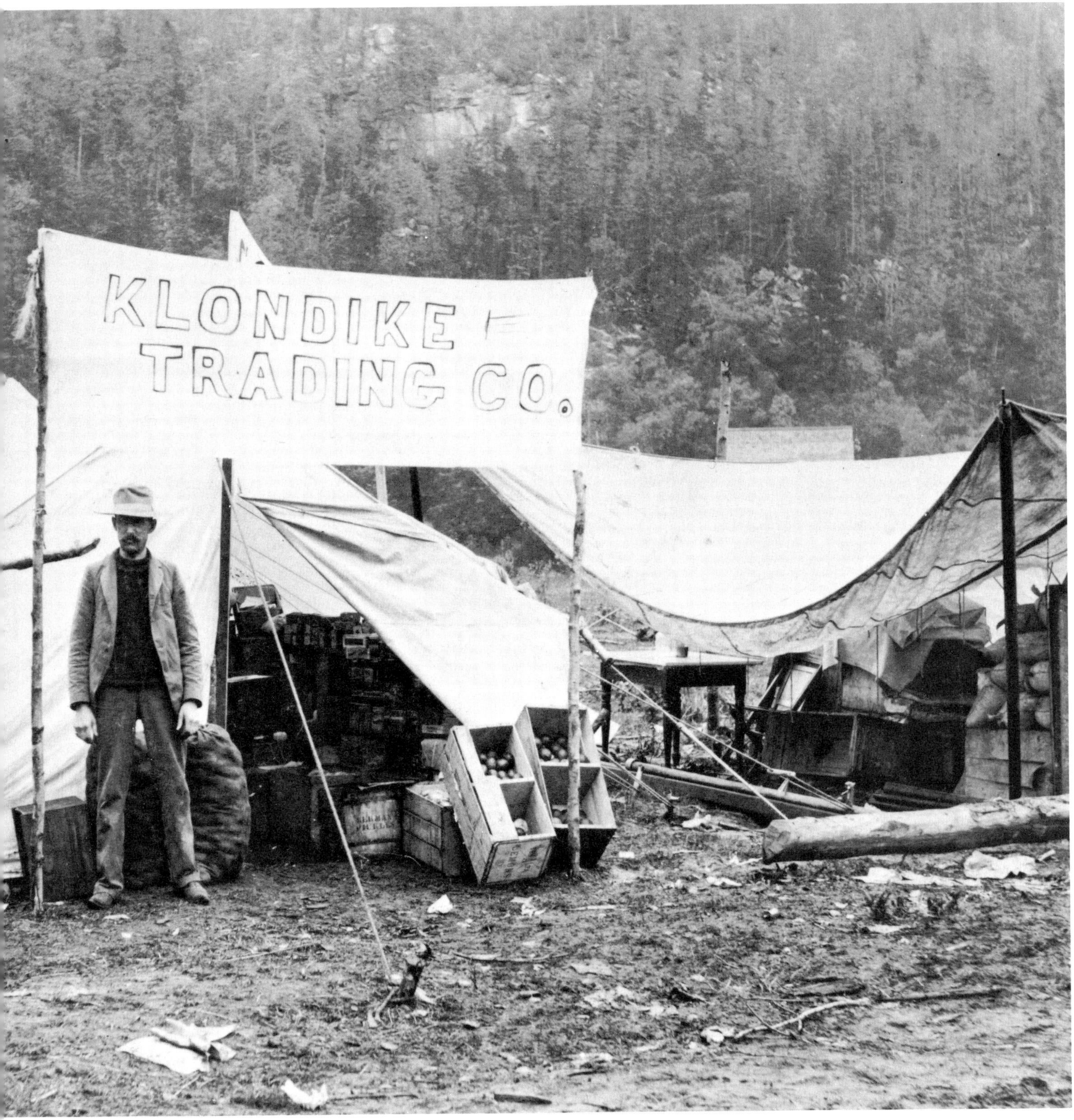
KLONDIKE
TRADING CO.

Business and Office Workers

AS AMERICAN INDUSTRIES turned out record numbers of goods, more and more workers were needed to run the businesses that these industries had created. Thousands of these employees were what we call "white-collar workers." That is, they worked in offices rather than in the factories where these goods were made. They were responsible for such things as keeping the financial records of the companies, taking orders for products, seeing that orders were filled, and seeing that the goods were shipped to the right places.

New inventions created all kinds of new jobs for office workers. Newly formed telephone companies employed thousands of people. So did telegraph offices and electric companies. Some of the new inventions were especially created to make office work more efficient. The typewriter, the dictating machine, and the adding machine made modern business methods possible. They helped create countless new jobs in American offices.

By 1900 American goods were being sold all over the world. Farm machinery was sold in Hungary, Russia, and Australia. Sewing machines were in use in both Europe and Asia. Typewriters and cash registers were sold everywhere.

American magazines and dime novels were filled with stories, real and imaginary, of people who had started out on the bottom rung of the business ladder and had made it to the top. Successful businessmen were true heroes of their day.

The telephone was invented in 1875. By 1900 there were nearly two million phones in the United States. Before long, America's telephone companies ranked among the largest employers in the nation.

The growth of banks in the United States kept pace with the rise of business. Actually they went hand in hand. The money that banks lent to businesses allowed the companies to grow. The earnings then put back into the banks by successful businessmen helped the banks become larger and more profitable. The banking profession attracted a great many people during this period. They were helped in their work by the use of the latest business machines.

In Her Own Words:
FROM SALESGIRL TO STENOGRAPHER

I GOT A JOB in one of the large department stores. I worked four months at selling pins, needles, thread, whalebone and a thousand and one other items. Then, by luck, I got a better job as a demonstrator of a new brand of coffee and tea in the grocery department of the same store.

But I did not want to be a coffee and tea demonstrator all my life. I had often thought I would like to learn shorthand and typewriting. I began to take a night course in stenography. I went to night school five nights out of every week. On Saturday night I did my washing and ironing. And on Sunday night I studied and read my textbooks.

When I had thoroughly learned the art of stenography and had attained the speed of over a hundred words a minute, I went to get a full-time job. I first had a job at $6 a week but soon got another one that paid $10. While I worked at this job I went back to night school, where I took a three-month's "speed course"! When I was done I got a job in a publishing house for $20 a week.

Here all of my studies bore fruit. Not only did I take dictation but soon other more important duties were passed my way. I even did some work usually reserved for editors. One day I mentioned to one of the editors some of the experiences I had gone through in working my way up from a salesgirl of needles and pins. After that I put an account of my experiences down on paper and to my surprise and delight they were accepted for publication in a magazine!

Adapted from *The Long Day*, Century Publishing Company, 1906.

Vanished Occupations

THE MEN, women, and children you have seen in this book were part of a labor force that played a vital role in building their nation. They worked at a time when, for the most part, working hours were longer and labor was more demanding than it is today. Nevertheless, they met their tasks and Americans are the richer for it.

Some of the jobs they worked at no longer exist. In the final pages of this book you will see people at work at what are now "vanished occupations." How many of these vanished occupations can you identify? (Answers on page 120.)

A

B

C

D

E

116

F

G

H

I

Vanished Occupations

A. Scissors grinder (This man sharpened scissors.)

B. Chimney sweeps (Workers like these cleaned out the thousands of chimneys in use in America at this time.)

C. Steeplejack (This skilled laborer painted and cleaned flagpoles and other ornaments atop high buildings.)

D. Ferryboat workers (This ferry was pulled from shore to shore by the cable.)

E. Ice cutters (In the days before refrigerators, ice was cut from lakes and ponds and used in iceboxes to keep food fresh.)

F. Feather-duster salesman (Millions of feather dusters were used each year to clean furniture, showcases, and the like.)

G. Stone crusher (The man is crushing stones by hand. He will then spread them over the road so that the road will be passable after heavy rains have turned the dirt into mud.)

H. Whalers (In this photograph the man atop the dead whale is about to attach a huge hook into the whale so that strips of blubber can be cut and hoisted aboard to be boiled down into oil.)

I. Lighthouse keeper (Today almost all lighthouses are electronically operated from central stations far from the lighthouse.)